THE HEROIN TRAIL

© Aladdin Books Ltd

Designed and produced by
Aladdin Books Ltd
70 Old Compton Street
London W1

First published in
Great Britain in 1986 by
Franklin Watts
12a Golden Square
London W1

ISBN 086313 483 1

The front cover photograph shows a girl injecting herself with heroin. The back cover photograph illustrates the conditions in which heroin is often used.

The author, Nigel Hawkes, is diplomatic correspondent of The Observer newspaper, London.

The consultant, Hugh Sykes, is a reporter for BBC Radio in London. He has reported extensively on heroin trafficking and heroin abuse in the United States and Pakistan.

Contents

THE HEROIN TRAIL

NIGEL HAWKES

Illustrated by

Ron Hayward Associates

Franklin Watts

London : New York : Toronto : Sydney

Introduction

Every day hundreds of thousands of people around the world, many of them young, are ruining their lives through heroin addiction. Most are damaged and many die as a result of this obsession. Heroin is a drug that brings little pleasure and a lot of pain. So why is it used and why are the numbers of addicts increasing?

Just as important, how is this situation possible? Heroin is an illegal drug: you can be sent to jail for selling it, or even for owning it. Yet heroin is available and is sold on street corners in every major town in the western world.

People are making vast profits out of trading in heroin. In the countries where it is made and the cities where it is sold, heroin changes hands for enormous amounts of money. The criminals who trade in it are getting rich. Why is this not being controlled? This book tries to answer these questions, by tracing the heroin trail from the field to the grave.

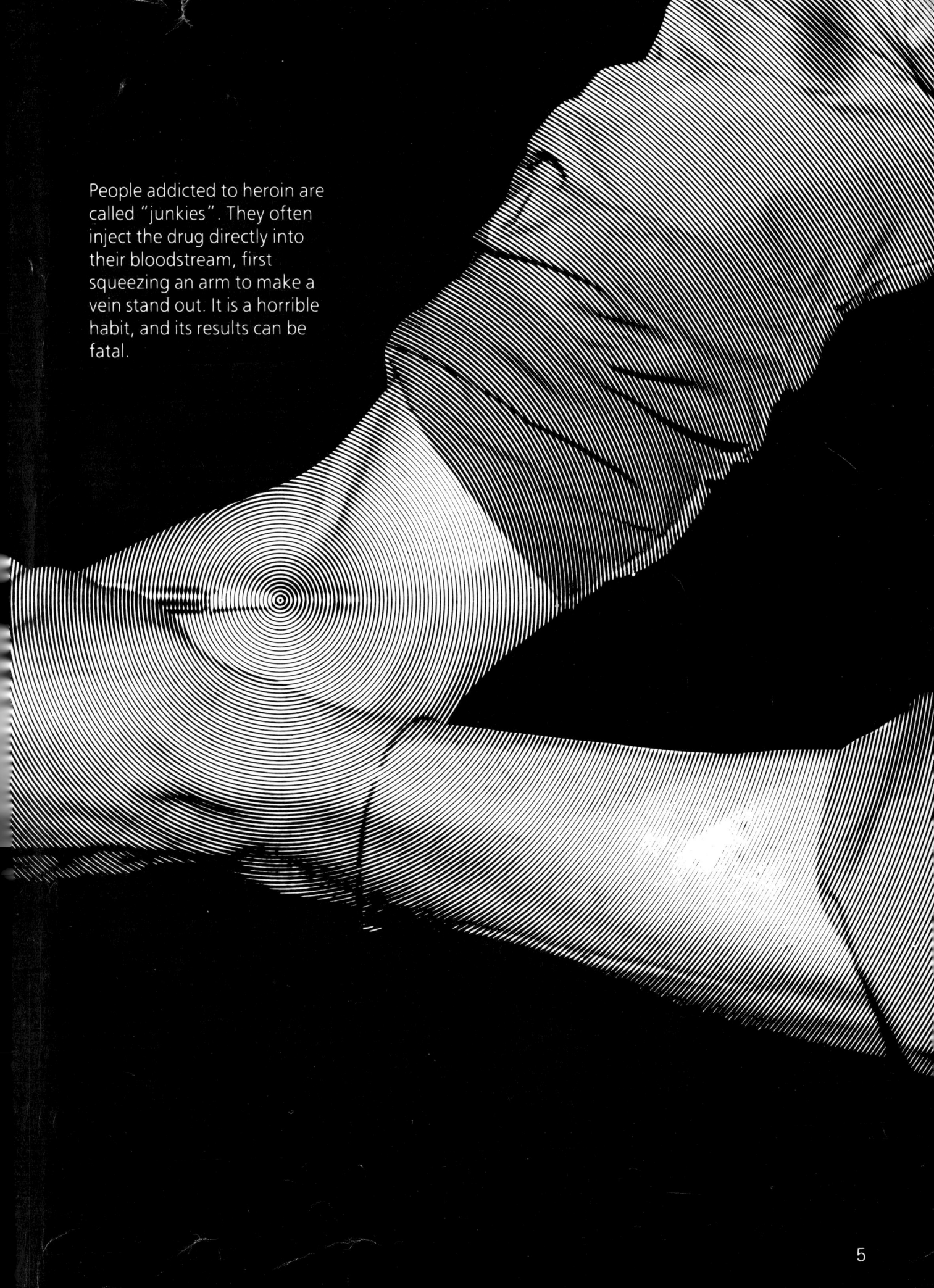

People addicted to heroin are called "junkies". They often inject the drug directly into their bloodstream, first squeezing an arm to make a vein stand out. It is a horrible habit, and its results can be fatal.

Drugs and drug abuse

Heroin is a drug — a chemical substance that alters a person's mood. Some drugs are legal, like alcohol, caffeine (in tea and coffee) and nicotine (in tobacco). Although both drinking and smoking can damage your health, these drugs are nevertheless permitted in western countries. In fact, they are an important source of revenue.

However many other drugs, including heroin, are illegal. These drugs are "controlled" — they cannot be sold without a doctor's prescription. They may have proper medical uses, or were originally produced by scientists trying to cure diseases or control pain.

When these drugs are habitually used for non-medical reasons by addicts — people who are dependent on drugs — we call this "drug abuse". Even possession of such drugs may be a criminal offence. Nevertheless, illegal drugs are widely produced, sold and used.

▽ Most drugs have been developed for medical purposes, like these pills and capsules. But if the effects they produce are pleasant or habit-forming, they too can become dangerously addictive and so become abused.

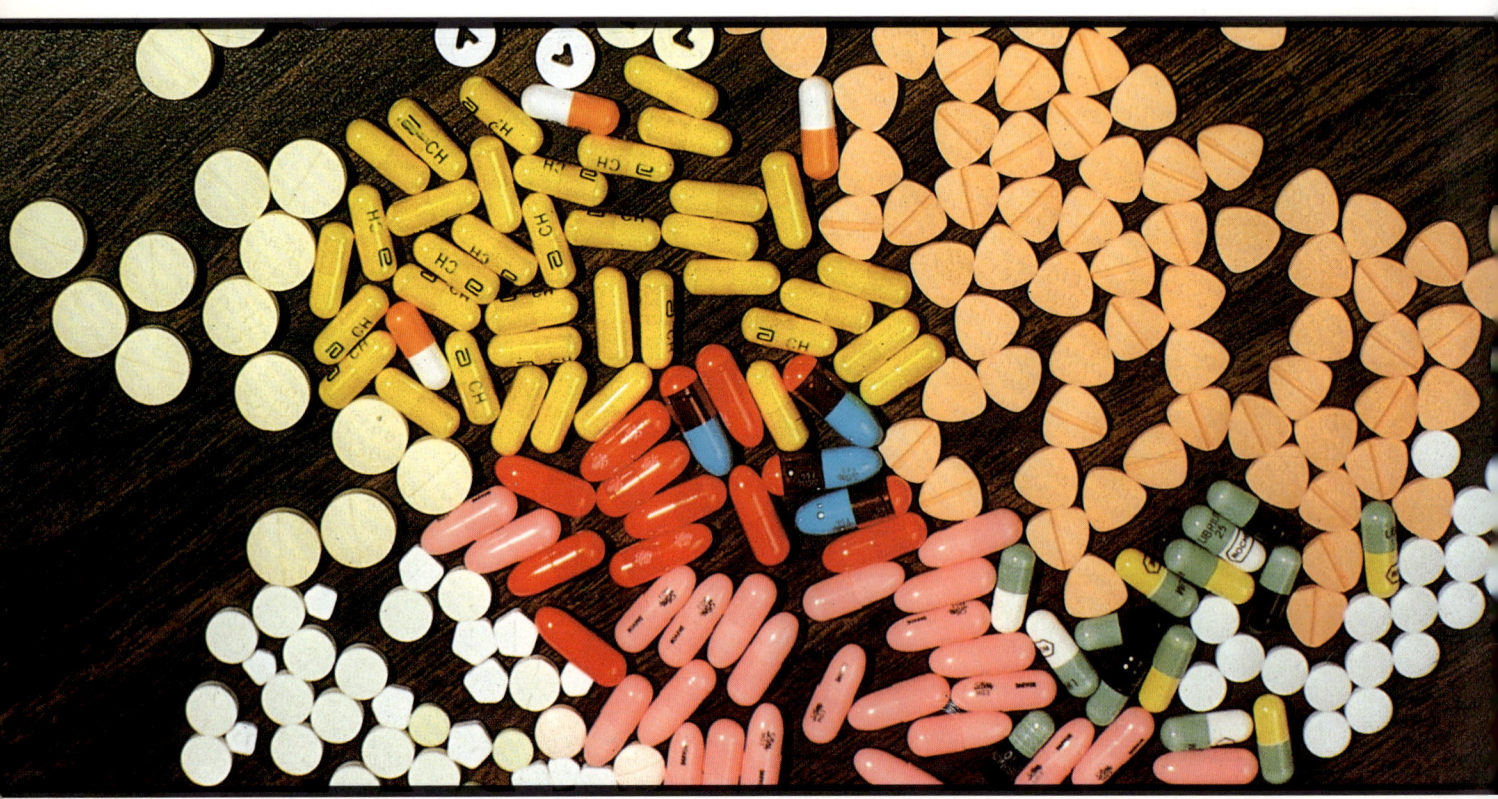

The range of drugs that is abused is vast. They may be pills to be swallowed, material to smoke or powders to be sniffed up the nose or injected. Heroin is among the most addictive of these drugs. It is a powder, usually white but sometimes beige or grey depending on its purity. Addicts inject it into their veins or into a muscle, smoke it or sniff it up a nostril.

The initial effect, they say, is a feeling of intense pleasure, followed by a much longer period of relaxed drowsiness. Heroin is a powerful painkiller, so its use brings relief from anxiety and pain. But this effect is only temporary – the effects wear off after a few hours. Because the addict's body is dependent on the drug, the addict is then left desperate for another injection. Such addiction has created and is also part of the heroin trail.

△ In some countries heroin is used in medicine, in sterile conditions, as a painkiller. However, most heroin is used illegally and often in conditions like those illustrated.

7

The poppy growers

The heroin trail begins with the farmer's story. Heroin comes from a plant, the opium poppy. A lot of opium is produced legally for medical use, but even more is grown secretly in remote areas where laws against it cannot be easily enforced.

The two most important opium-growing areas are the so-called "Golden Triangle" on the borders between Thailand and Burma, and the "Golden Crescent", a mountainous region on the border between Afghanistan and the North West Frontier Province of Pakistan.

Here, in the dry and barren soil, only two crops are possible – wheat or opium poppies. On an average family landholding wheat produces only £10 a year, but poppies bring as much as £300. There are frequent raids by the military and the frontier police to stop this illegal poppy growing. However, farmers continue to harvest poppies, ensuring a steady supply of opium to be manufactured into heroin.

▷ In fields in the remote corners of the Golden Triangle, farmers tend the growing poppies. In some places the soil is so barren that opium poppies are the *only* crop which will grow.

▽ Calculating the total harvest of the two main poppy-growing regions is largely guesswork. But we know that since 1980 the Golden Crescent has become the more important.

Golden Crescent: 1983 — 1,238 tonnes

Golden Triangle: 1983 — 675 tonnes

Opium growing regions

Iran · Afghanistan · Pakistan · Burma · Laos · Thailand

From plants to drugs

The first part of the process involved in manufacturing heroin is performed by the farmer, who makes cuts in the seed pods of the poppies. A milky white juice oozes from these cuts. This is opium. Within a few days it hardens and darkens to form a sticky, brown substance which can be scraped off and sold ready for the next stage in the manufacturing process.

Opium itself is a dangerously addictive drug. "Opium dens", where people lie listlessly on bunk-beds smoking opium, can still be found in parts of the Far East. Today, however, most opium is converted into heroin. This actually requires little skill or knowledge. Heroin can be produced by a couple of chemists using fairly basic equipment.

The poppy on the right is scarred by the cuts made to remove the opium. It takes only simple chemistry to convert the opium from the seed pod of the poppy into the white powder of heroin.

Legal heroin is produced in sparkling clean laboratories under sterile conditions. But the much greater amounts produced illegally are made in very crude surroundings.

In hidden primitive laboratories, raw opium is mixed with water to which lime has been added. This produces a form of "morphine", a powerful drug which is immensely useful in medicine as a painkiller. Boiling morphine with a common industrial chemical produces heroin. Ten kilogrammes (22 lbs) of opium will make one kilogramme (2.2 lbs) of heroin.

Sometimes police find these hidden laboratories and destroy them. But because the equipment is simple and not expensive, a new laboratory can be quickly set up and production re-established. In 1983, for example, the Pakistan police destroyed 41 laboratories. Yet figures suggest that heroin production nevertheless continued without a pause.

△ Pakistan's North West Frontier police show off what they say was an illegal heroin laboratory: a few crates, old oil drums, and sacks of raw materials. This was a successful close-down — but the heroin producers no doubt moved on somewhere else.

On the smuggler's trail

Smugglers appear to be able to move heroin along the trail with few problems. Heroin is quite openly sold to drug dealers at, for example, the small towns of Landi Kotal on the Khyber Pass, or Mae Hong Son on the border between Thailand and Burma. The dealers then smuggle the heroin onwards to the big cities where there are flights to Europe and the United States.

Part of the smuggler's success is because heroin is light, compact and easy to hide. However, success is also due to the ease with which officials in poor countries like Thailand or Pakistan are bribed. For a payoff, either in money or drugs, many officials will look the other way or tip off the heroin traders when a police raid is about to happen.

▽ Farmers from the Golden Triangle sell their raw opium. It is loaded onto ponies by a smuggler ready for the trip to market. The smuggler is armed. However, it seems that the journey from field to market to laboratory contains few difficulties.

No matter how hard a line a government wants to take on the heroin trail, their task is made extremely difficult by bribery and corruption.

In 1982 the Thai Army launched an attack against the biggest drug warlord in the Golden Triangle, Khun Sa (1). A heavily-armed detachment of men marched on the remote region on the Burmese border where Khun Sa rules.

Khun Sa was no doubt warned of the attack. He is well armed and defended by a private army (2) and the attack consequently failed. But in a fierce battle 17 government soldiers and 80 of Khun Sa's men were killed and a village was destroyed (3). Khun Sa himself escaped to continue the heroin trade.

On to the streets

At every stage of heroin's journey, somebody makes a profit. Heroin that costs £5,000 a kilogramme in Pakistan can be sold on the streets of Europe or the United States for at least £60,000. It is carried there, usually by air, by "couriers". They are the link whose job is simply to pick up heroin in the Far East or in India or Pakistan and fly it to Europe or the United States.

At each stage, the heroin is "cut" – mixed with other substances which range from glucose to even brick dust. Normally the heroin bought in Pakistan is 70 per cent pure, but by the time it reaches the streets it has been cut to a purity of only about 35 per cent.

As a result the profits made are huge. In Britain they probably amount to about £250 million a year, in the United States several times as much. Of this, the big importers who finance the business but have nothing to do with street distribution take perhaps as much as £50 million.

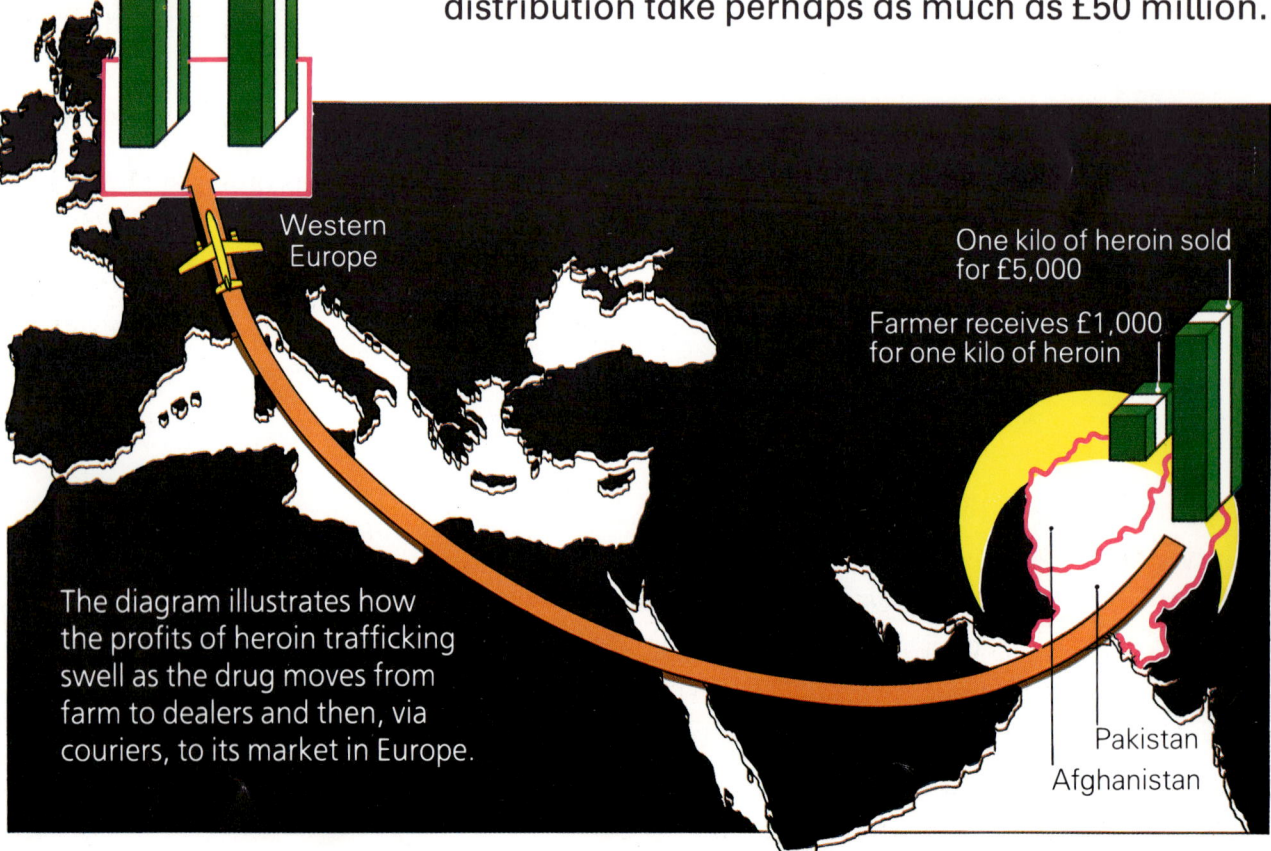

One kilo of heroin separated and sold on street for £60,000+

One kilo of heroin sold for £20,000

Western Europe

One kilo of heroin sold for £5,000

Farmer receives £1,000 for one kilo of heroin

Pakistan

Afghanistan

The diagram illustrates how the profits of heroin trafficking swell as the drug moves from farm to dealers and then, via couriers, to its market in Europe.

Some of the enormous profits made from heroin smuggling are deposited in banks in countries like Switzerland. Here many bank accounts are absolutely secret. There is some evidence to suggest that money is processed even when its origins are known. Often the money is "laundered" — it is illegally passed through legitimate businesses so that its origins cannot easily be traced.

Even at street level profits continue to be made. Most heroin is bought from other heroin addicts, usually those with a much heavier addiction, using as much as a gramme of heroin a day. Such addicts can only afford their habit if they can acquire a lot of money, and the easiest way to do that is to deal in heroin. Consequently many addicts also operate as dealers.

△ A typical addict uses about a fifth of a gramme a day, sold on street corners in £5 or £10 bags. On the streets of Paris, an addict is photographed buying a bag of heroin from a dealer. The furtive exchange is over in seconds.

The networks

◁ A victim of the "heroin wars" of the early 1980s, Paolo Bevilacqua was shot dead as he sat at an open-air cafe in Palermo, Sicily on 31 July, 1982.

▽ In 1986, a massive trial of Mafia members opened. Here Mafia defendants facing charges of drug trafficking, murder and extortion, sit behind bars in the "bunker", a specially built courthouse in Palermo, Sicily.

Heroin smuggling networks are controlled by powerful criminals. They seldom handle the drug. All they do is order and pay for it, and then collect the profits.

These networks are efficient and contain ruthless people. Big Pakistani dealers use an Asian network. Chinese syndicates are heavily involved, as are the Italian Mafia.

The Mafia, a Sicilian crime ring with direct connections to organised crime in the United States, does not hesitate to kill if its operations are threatened. In the early 1980s the killings mounted, as judges, officials, police officers and other members of the Mafia were slaughtered in battles to preserve and control the trade.

Why heroin?

The massive profits made by the drug networks would not exist unless there were a huge demand for their product. There are half a million heroin addicts in the United States, at least 50,000 in Britain, and the numbers are going up fast. Why?

Generally, people take drugs to escape from reality. If life is hard or dull, users may think that heroin provides excitement. If social conditions are difficult – if there is high unemployment or little money – users may think that heroin provides escape. Moreover, heroin today is cheap and easily available. For some people this is enough reason to try it. Others may be tempted because they feel pressure from friends.

However, whatever the original reason a person has to choose heroin, it usually results in there being no choice. The final reason to use heroin is that the user is addicted: heroin has become a necessity.

▷ A young girl heroin addict "crashes out" into a deep sleep after taking the drug. Today there are hundreds of thousands of addicts like her.

▽ Those most at risk from heroin are teenagers, facing all the problems and anxieties of growing up. The graph illustrates the dramatic increase in young heroin users in Britain since 1976.

1976 1978 1980 1982 1984

The toll

The price of heroin addiction is heavy, but is often misunderstood. Heroin *itself* does not kill, even if it is taken for a lifetime. It is the pattern of life created by addiction, the risks of infection and disease from dirty needles, the dangers of an accidental overdose and the dirt and neglect that come with addiction that claim lives. It is estimated that within five years of becoming addicted to heroin, one in six addicts is dead.

The effects of heroin addiction are social as well as physical. Addicts may stop eating, lose weight, and appear yellow and jaundiced. In addition, many become withdrawn and unsociable. The drug becomes the centre of their lives and they abandon family and friends. Many turn to crime in order to get the money to buy heroin, not just dealing, but also stealing from their own families or from other addicts.

Addiction is a horrible way of life. Getting money, buying drugs and taking them are the only things that matter. Heroin totally controls the addict's life.

▽ Heroin addiction and its links with crime make headlines all around the world. Most countries suffer from it; none has yet found an answer.

'Woman stole to pay for heroin'

A WOMAN who stole to pay for heroin was remanded in custody until 15 May by Rochdale magistrates on Monday.

Heroin addict robbed uncle

A MAN of 20 was so addicted to heroine he committed a string of offences to satisfy his craving, was told...

Addict denies killing baby

They were given regular

I trafficanti l'avevano abbandonata 3 mesi fa
Due miliardi di eroina in una valigia lasciata nella stazione di Napoli
D'AVANZO
...s la lutte anti- drogue.

se non lo confermano in modo ufficiale, sono convinti che il corriere sia stato ucciso. Anzi, pare che stiano lavorando su

TRAPPED BY EVI WEB OF HEROIN

...DICT Hugh Clark ...und himself trapped ...a vicious circle ...en he became ...oked on heroin.

...o pay the evil pushers for ...drug he craved, Clark ...rrowed from money-

Addict stole for drugs

560 Paisley Road West, Ibrox, turned to crime. He raided for jewellery, cas video tapes an Clark ad breaking. Glasgow's 26 and Oct

On other occasions, he got in through windows and a door which ...ng had not been left properly secured

PUSHERS
...last raid neighbours ...wo men walking ...ag and

Mr Gilchrist said the goods not recovered £2500

Mr Peter Gellatly, de the accused, who liv com law wife bec ated

Kopstuk he hoort tien
il co

The shivers, shakes and finally the fix

Teena

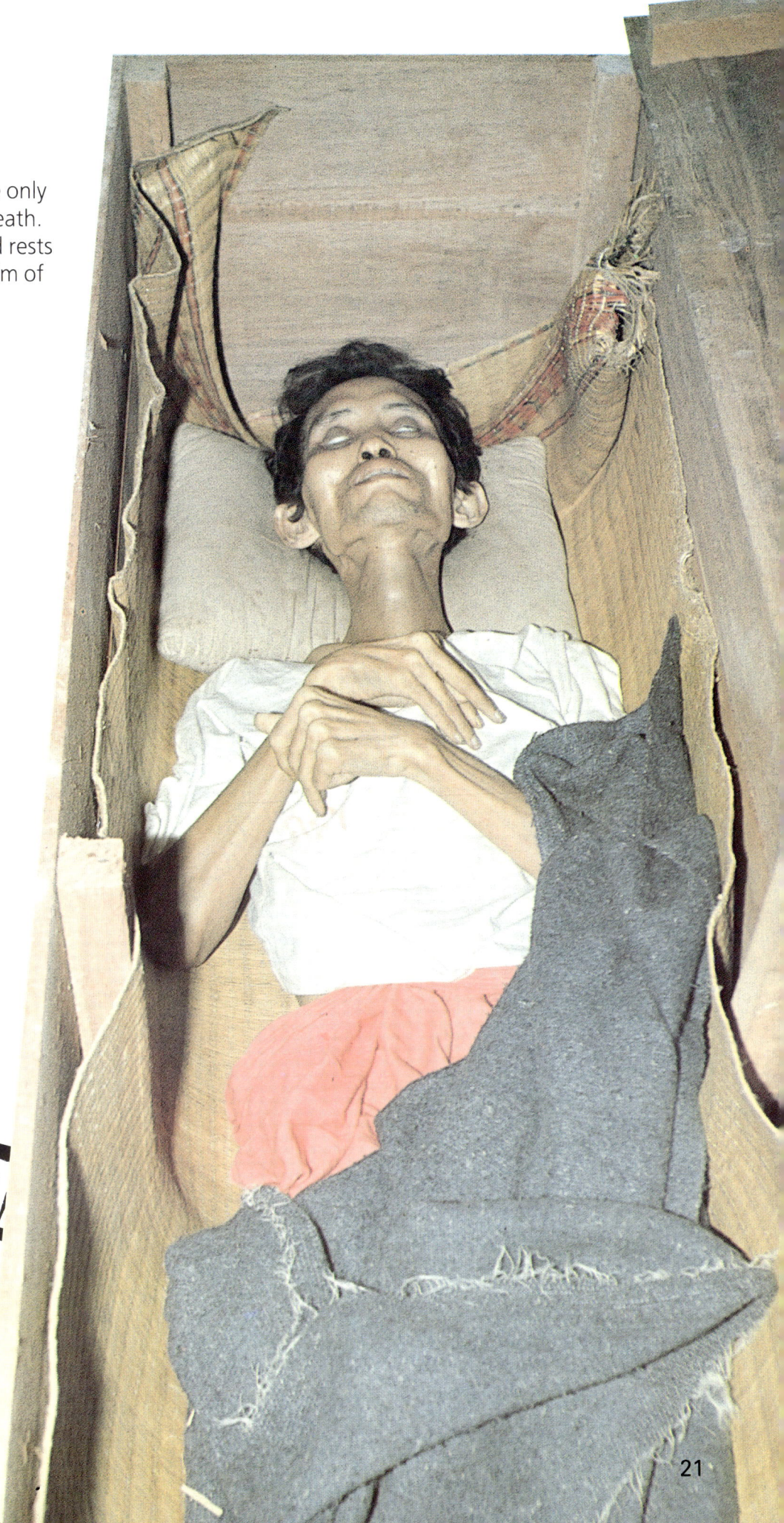

▷ For many addicts the only escape from heroin is death. An addict from Thailand rests in a simple coffin, a victim of his addiction.

deux trafiquants
interpellés

**LES MOUCHA
ANTI-DROGUE
ARRIVENT**

umo di eroina,

inehandel

Coming clean

Heroin addiction can be beaten, but not easily. Because of the difficulty of "coming clean" – giving up heroin – there are several different opinions on how to treat heroin addiction.

For example, some doctors prescribe a heroin substitute called methadone to ease withdrawal symptoms. (Withdrawal symptoms consist of a week or so of feeling very ill, rather like a bad bout of flu, when an addict first stops taking heroin.) Other doctors, however, feel that giving methadone to a heroin addict is like treating an alcoholic with more alcohol.

It has even been suggested by a few (and condemned by many) that heroin be made legal in an effort to better control its use and so help addicts. Yet despite these differing opinions, it is agreed by all that long-term support is needed to help addicts trying to come clean.

△ In Warsaw, Poland, medical aid comes to an addict who has collapsed on a wall after taking an overdose of heroin. Inset, former addict William O'Donnell, who runs a rehabilitation centre for addicts in the United States, embraces one of his patients.

Unfortunately help is not always available. There are private clinics for those who can afford them, and some specialist drug centres (though not enough). Some addicts have to face the tough task of coming off heroin in prison.

Many addicts try repeatedly to come clean, without success. But studies show that many do succeed. In the United Kingdom, for example, 40 per cent were still using drugs ten years after coming to a treatment centre, but another 40 per cent were not. The rest were dead.

▽ Choose life not drugs: the slogan of an anti-drug campaign run by the Scottish Health Education Group designed to persuade addicts to "come clean".

CHOOSE LIFE Not DRUGS

DRUGS AND YOUNG PEOPLE IN SCOTLAND

DRUG MISUSE A REGISTER OF HELPING AGENCIES

BE ALL YOU CAN BE
Issued by the Scottish Health Education Group

Busting the pushers

The police could arrest heroin addicts easily if they wanted to, but it would not solve the problem. Instead they try to break the supply chain by arresting pushers, or dealers, and traffickers – people who distribute drugs – before they can snare more people into addiction.

However, ensuring that the pushers do not return to the streets is difficult. Success at catching traffickers is also limited. Sniffer dogs can be used to detect heroin at ports and airports, but there can never be enough customs men to search everybody. Customs men consequently believe that they are intercepting just a fraction of the heroin being smuggled. So despite all attempts at this level, the supply of heroin can always meet the demand.

▷ Every year the arrest rate for offences involving heroin rises, as more and more people are drawn into drug-taking. In the foreground, a New York policeman arrests a man suspected of drug offences.

▽ A sniffer dog at a Florida airport checks the luggage on a conveyor belt. Dogs can be trained to sniff out drugs even inside suitcases.

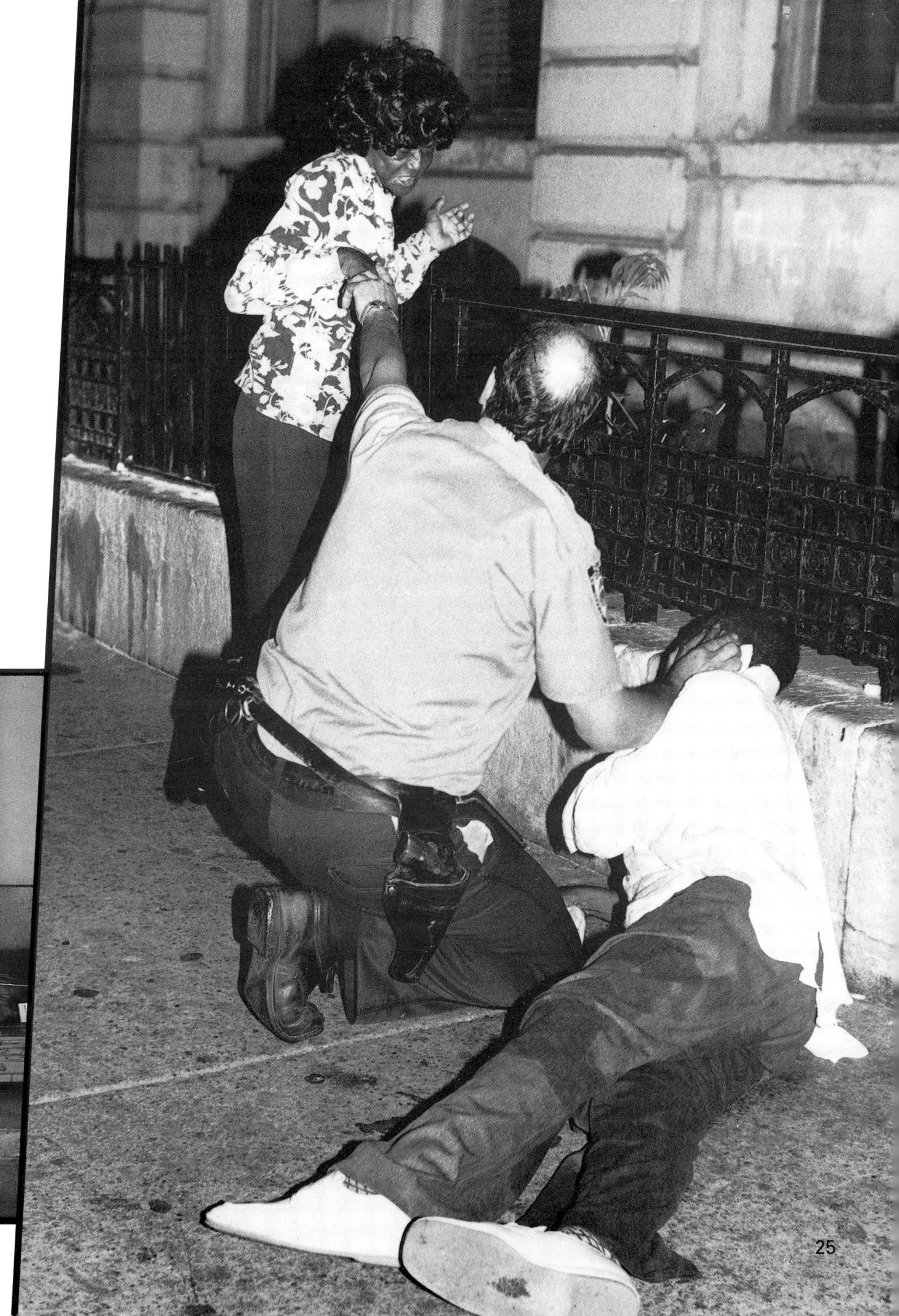

Hitting the networks

A more effective way to break the trail is to hit the networks. Organised crime must be beaten if the drug trade is to be controlled.

Drug specialists have now been based in many western embassies abroad to collect information about the drug networks and send it back to coastguards and police. They can then arrest couriers, and seize the heroin before it gets to the distributors. Or couriers can be followed to reveal the dealers they are working for.

These methods have had some success. But the profits to be made by smuggling drugs are so huge that they will always attract criminals. In an effort to control these profits, some countries, like Britain, are introducing laws to take away the property of convicted smugglers.

▽ American coastguards make a successful arrest of drug smugglers. A lot of drugs enter the United States smuggled in small boats.

5,606 kg

1,708 kg

546 kg

| 1968 | 1975 | 1981 |

World seizures

915 kg

359 kg

183 kg

| 1968 | 1975 | 1981 |

American seizures
(including Mexico and
Canada)

1,094 kg

311 kg

12 kg

| 1968 | 1975 | 1981 |

European seizures

Heroin seizures are rising.
Unfortunately, the
increase is due to more
heroin being smuggled,
as well as to improved
control methods. In the
US seizures have actually
fallen. Seized heroin is
sometimes burned.

A global problem

Today governments everywhere recognise that drugs are a problem and are attempting to deal with heroin abuse in various ways. Some have introduced tough new penalties, including death, for those convicted of trafficking in drugs. For example, in Malaysia in 1983 two Australians were condemned to death for trying to carry heroin through the airport at Kuala Lumpur.

Poppy farmers are being paid money to shift to alternative crops. In Pakistan a big effort has been made to persuade the growers to plant other crops. Money from western governments and the United Nations provides the crops, plus irrigation to make them grow. Several countries around the world have also launched campaigns and education schemes to persuade young people to steer clear of drugs.

▽ Nancy Reagan, America's First Lady, has campaigned hard to persuade young people in the United States to reject drugs. Here she is talking to a group of children at a special conference she organised on drug abuse.

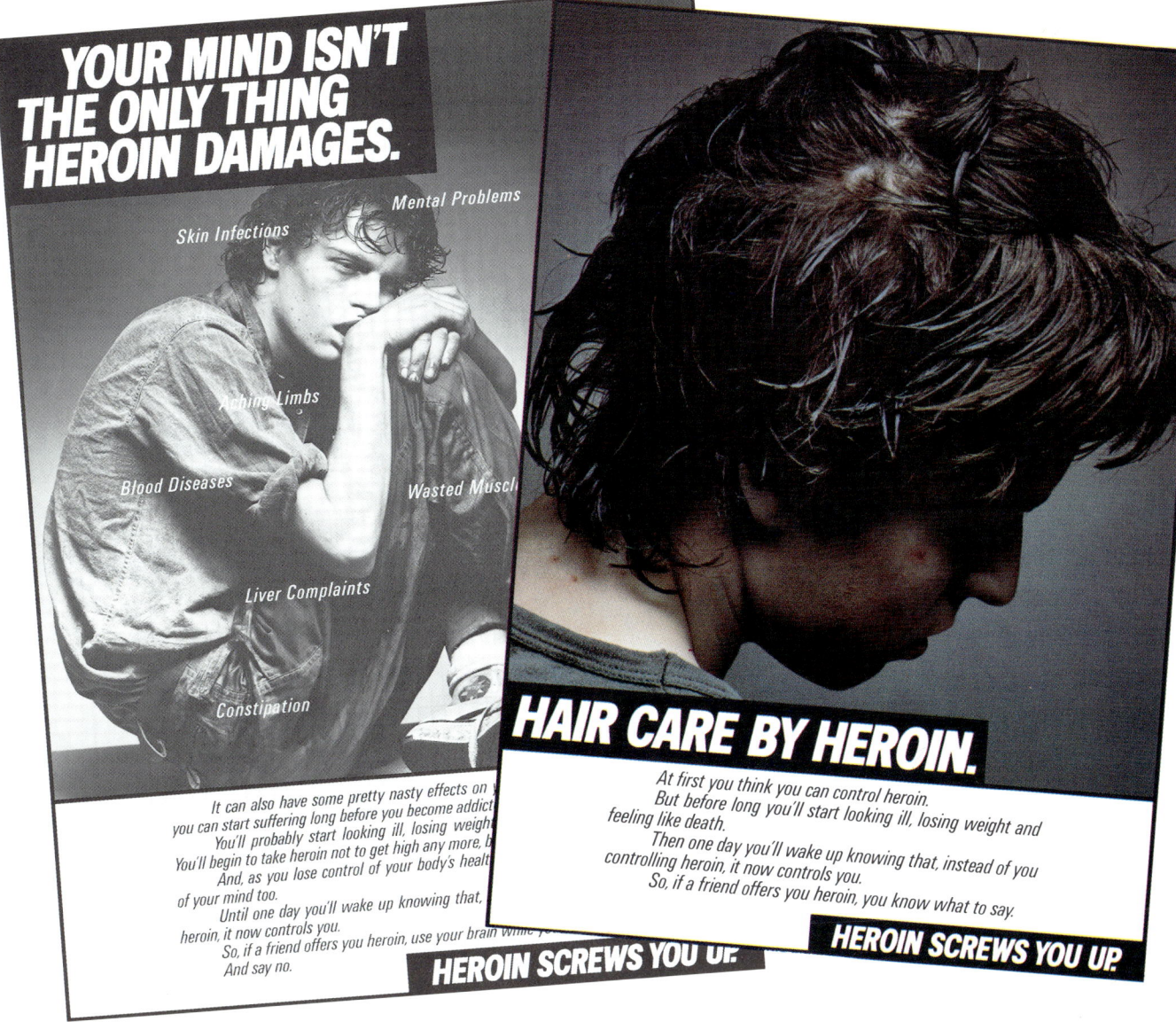

YOUR MIND ISN'T THE ONLY THING HEROIN DAMAGES.

Mental Problems

Skin Infections

Aching Limbs

Blood Diseases

Wasted Muscle

Liver Complaints

Constipation

It can also have some pretty nasty effects on you can start suffering long before you become addict
You'll probably start looking ill, losing weigh
You'll begin to take heroin not to get high any more, b
And, as you lose control of your body's health
of your mind too.
Until one day you'll wake up knowing that,
heroin, it now controls you.
So, if a friend offers you heroin, use your brain while
And say no.

HEROIN SCREWS YOU UP.

HAIR CARE BY HEROIN.

At first you think you can control heroin.
But before long you'll start looking ill, losing weight and
feeling like death.
Then one day you'll wake up knowing that, instead of you
controlling heroin, it now controls you.
So, if a friend offers you heroin, you know what to say.

HEROIN SCREWS YOU UP.

△ Nobody is forced to become a heroin addict. The British government has launched an advertising campaign aimed at young people. It is designed to warn them of the effects of heroin addiction. If it saves even a few lives, many consider that it will be worth the £2 million a year it is costing.

In 1987 the United Nations is to hold a major conference on Drug Abuse and Illicit Trafficking in the hope of improving the odds of catching smugglers and destroying the menace of drugs.

However, if we are to prevent more lives, especially those of young people, being damaged or destroyed by heroin, something more than these efforts will have to be made. The combination of huge profits and the awful hold the drug can gain over so many people makes the problems posed by the heroin trail very difficult. Supply can always meet demand. And so perhaps in the end, the solution will depend on creating a society in which young people can find the strength and determination to say no to heroin and other drugs.

Chronology

4000 BC The opium poppy is known to the Sumerians, who call it the "plant of joy".

1805 The German apothecary Frederick Serturner isolates morphine from opium.

1840 Britain, the major supplier of opium to China from India, fights a war to be allowed to continue the supply. Britain wins, and China cedes the island of Hong Kong.

1856 The second Opium War takes place. Britain wins again and expands the opium trade to China. It is a major source of income. China has up to 15 million opium addicts.

1874 Heroin is discovered in London by C.R. Alder-Wright, more or less by accident, during a series of experiments in which he mixed morphine with various chemicals.

1898 Bayer, the German chemical company, begins the commercial production of heroin, and markets it as a sedative for coughs. It is also thought to "cure" morphine addiction.

1912 The First International Narcotics Convention in The Hague, Netherlands agrees new controls on the growing of opium poppies.

1920 The Dangerous Drugs Act in the UK limits the use of heroin to bona-fide medical treatment. However, doctors continue to prescribe morphine and heroin to perhaps 500 addicts.

1920s and 30s Heroin addiction grows more rapidly in the US, where heroin is illegal. Organised crime gets involved.

1960s The Vietnam War exposes many US servicemen to heroin produced in the Golden Triangle. Drug-taking of all types increases, but heroin addiction in Britain is still limited to about 2,500 addicts.

1979 The Iranian Revolution sends a wave of cheap heroin across Europe, encouraging more addiction.

1980-86 Heroin addiction in Europe grows rapidly, fed by large quantities of cheap, good quality heroin from the Golden Crescent. There are up to 60,000 heroin addicts in the United Kingdom by 1986.

Numbers of registered addicts worldwide, 1983

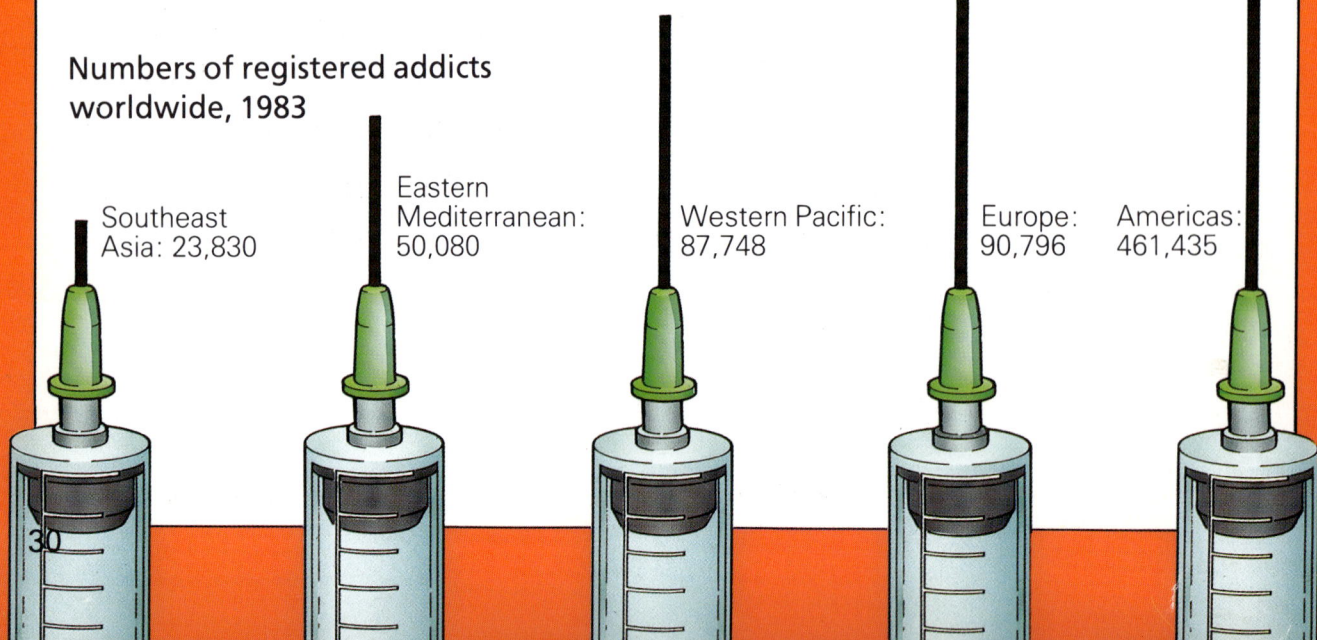

Southeast Asia: 23,830

Eastern Mediterranean: 50,080

Western Pacific: 87,748

Europe: 90,796

Americas: 461,435

Hard facts on a hard drug

"   I wake early. The sun is shining but to me it's just another lousy day. I eat but the sickness overtakes me. Every morning I get it, unless I can fix up before it strikes, but I can't today because I've no money and no heroin.

I shiver feverishly, clutching at the blankets in an effort to reduce the pain. I pretend to be asleep so that my mother won't notice how sick I am....

Finally I make it into town and head towards the room where the others hang out. I see that some of the others have already fixed up. They've got the record player on. The trick is to make everything appear normal....

I'm getting the rush* now. I made it today. I got high before cold turkey** took over. When I get home, I stagger upstairs. I close my eyes and sleep, ready for another lousy day tomorrow, knowing my life is ruled by heroin and what will happen if I don't get a fix. I can't see an end to the familiar routine, unless I don't wake up tomorrow. "

* sensation of pleasure
  immediately after injection
** withdrawal symptoms   *A. M., aged 17 years*

Index

Photographic Credits:
Cover and pages 6 and 22: Magnum/John Hillelson; pages 4-5, 9, 10, 12, 13, 15, 16, 17, 25, 26, 27 and 28: Frank Spooner; pages 7, 19, 22 and back cover: Rex Features; page 10: David Hoffman; page 18: Art Directors; page 21: Hutchinson; page 23: Scottish Education Office; page 24: Colorific; page 29: Dept of Health and Social Security.

PRINTED IN BELGIUM BY

proost
INTERNATIONAL BOOK PRODUCTION